BAR M

MW01295101

by
Anonymous

from the
Maine Republic Email Alert
3 Linnell Circle
Brunswick, Maine 04011

www.mainerepublicemailalert.com

CONTENTS

This book provides you with documented evidence of the following facts AND MORE:

3

Defending Liberty
Pursuing Justice

AMERICAN BAR ASSOCIATION

All BAR members are foreign Agents of the Crown

Posted on April 1, 2017 by Anonymous request.

After Recording, return to;
Glenn Winningham; house of Fearn
Non-domestic Mail
C/O 6340 Lake Worth Blvd. #437
Fort Worth, Texas republic
ZIP CODE EXEMPT
DMM 602.1.3.e.2,
18 USC § 1342

BAR Member Affidavit
(All BAR members are foreign agents of the Crown)

Arizona republic	)
	) Subscribed, Sworn, Sealed
Pinal County	)

I, Me, My, or Myself, also known as Glenn Winningham; house of Fearn, having been duly put under oath, I do affirm, depose, and being cognizant of the penalties for bearing false witness, do declare that;

All the Facts stated herein are true, correct, complete, are not hearsay, are not misleading, but are admissible as evidence, and if called to testify, I shall so State, and further,

I have standing capacity to act, as to the lawful matters stated herein, and further,

I have personal, firsthand knowledge, and executive and documented knowledge of the facts stated herein, and further,

I am currently an inhabitant of the land sometimes known as "Texas", on Turtle island, and I have no firsthand knowledge of My date nor place of birth. Any evidence anywhere about My birth is hearsay evidence and inadmissible evidence in any court because both of My parents and the attending physician involved in My entry into this world are now dead and I have not had an opportunity to cross-examine them in court to determine the veracity of any evidence they may have been able to provide. Having said that, I do remember that I finished high school in the year one thousand nine hundred and seventy-five, almost forty years ago, therefore I am well past the age of majority, and further,

I am a Sovereign Living Soul and a Holder of the Office of "the People", and a Judicial Power Citizen by right of blood as described in the Corporate Denial Affidavit # 062013 which is recorded with the Pinal County Recorder at Fee Number 2013-032373, and all subsequent superseding documents, *all of which is incorporated herein by reference in its entirety, and all of which is now the unrebutted truth, and public policy,* and further,

I am not in the military, and further,

The use of any statutes, codes, rules, regulations, or court citations, within any document created by Me at any time, is only to notice that which is applicable to government officials, and is not intended, nor shall it be construed, to mean that I have conferred, submitted to, or entered into any jurisdiction alluded to thereby, and further,

Equality under the Law is paramount and mandatory by Law, and further,

The purpose of this document is to establish the fact that all BAR members are foreign agents of the Vatican, and are therefore enemy agents, but first we must establish that BAR members are all foreign agents of the Crown, and;

the Crown is a corporation domiciled in the City of London, in England, and;

the Crown has nothing to do with Queen Elizabeth, because if it were Queen Elizabeth's Crown, it would have an "ER" superimposed over it, which stands for "Elizabeth Regina", and;

the City of London is foreign to the rest of England, just as the District of Columbia is foreign to the rest of the united States of America.

"The United States Government is a foreign corporation with respect to a State of the Union." — In Re Merriam's Estate, 36 N.E. 505, 141 N.Y. 479, affirmed 16 S.Ct. 1073, 41 L.Ed. 287, and;

the City of London is a walled-in part of downtown London, England, approximately two square miles, and there are 12 gates, and it contains the Imperial Parliament buildings, and;

William the Conqueror conquered all of England, except for the City of London, and;

periodically they show the convening of the imperial

parliament on television, and it is very "telling" about the nature of the City of London, because the Queen goes to one of the gates called "Temple BAR", which is essentially a big oak door, with a small one foot square door in it, and both doors are closed, and the Queen beats on the door with her scepter, and the Lord Mayor of London (on the other side of the door) opens the small door and asks the Queen what she wants, and she has to get permission to enter the foreign territory of the City of London, and while she is in there she walks 2 steps behind the Lord Mayor of London, and with her head bowed, because she is not a sovereign in there, and;

there are four law schools in the City of London, and one of them is called Inns of Court...

"INNS OF COURT – These are certain private unincorporated associations, in the nature of collegiate houses, located in the City of London, and invested with the exclusive privilege of calling men to the bar..." — Black's Law Dictionary, 5th Edition page 709. [emphasis added], and,

there is an American Inns of Court, and there are chapters in every state in America, therefore all BAR members owe their allegiance to the Inns of Court, which is a foreign power, and further,

The City of London and the Crown are both owned and operated by the Vatican, as found in the Concession to the Pope (1213), in which King John agreed to pay tribute to the Vatican;

"We wish it to be known to all of you, through this our charter, furnished with our seal, that... we... do offer

and freely concede to... our mother the holy Roman church, and to our lord pope Innocent and to his Catholic successors, the whole kingdom of England and the whole kingdom Ireland, with all their rights and appurtenances... As a sign, moreover, of this our own, we will and establish perpetual obligation and concession, and we will and establish that from the proper and especial revenues of our aforesaid kingdoms, for all the service and customs which we ought to render for them... the Roman church shall receive yearly a thousand marks sterling, namely at the feast of St. Michael five hundred marks, and at Easter five hundred marks-seven hundred, namely, for the kingdom of England, and three hundred for the kingdom of Ireland..." — Concessions to the Pope (1213),

because "we the people" of England revolted against the tyrant King John, therefore the tyrant could NOT make his payments, and therefore had to go bankrupt, and all corporations become the property of the creditors in a bankruptcy;

"Under the US Airways proposal sent in November, AMR creditors would own 70 percent and US Airways shareholders 30 percent of the merged airline, which could be valued at around $8.5 billion, sources told Reuters on Friday." — AMR Creditors Prefer all Stock Merger with US Airways: sources, by Soyoung Kim, Reuters, Wednesday 12 December 2012 8:38 PM EST, taken from Yahoo Finance [emphasis added],

therefore it is effectively a coup de tat, and the Crown, and the City of London are now owned and operated by the Vatican, and further,

11

Because King John needed to raise money to pay the Vatican, he imposed martial law rule; and there are three kinds of Martial Law;

   i.   Full Martial Law – Soldiers on the streets used ONLY in a foreign country,or to put down an insurrection.
   ii.   Martial Law Proper – the law of the Armed forces.
   iii.   Martial Law Rule – the law of necessity and emergency used during peace times. — Ex Parte Milligan 4 Wall (71 U.S.) 2, 18 L.Ed. 281, p 302, [emphasis added]

The law of emergency and necessity was used to impose martial law rule in England in 1213, just like criminals in the United States use the law of emergency and necessity to impose martial law rule today;
"It is an established fact that the United States Federal Government has been dissolved by the Emergency Banking Act, March 9, 1933, 48 stat. 1, Public Law 89-719; declared by President Roosevelt, being bankrupt and insolvent, H.J.R. 192, 73rd Congress in session June 5, 1933 – Joint Resolution To Suspend The Gold Standard and Abrogate The Gold Clause dissolved the Sovereign Authority of the United States and the official capacities of all United States Governmental Offices, Officers, and Departments, and is further evidence that the United States Federal Government exists today in name only." United States Congressional Record, March 17, 1993 Vol. 33 [Emphasis added].

"Since March 9, 1933, the United States has been in a state of declared National Emergency . . . Under the

powers delegated by these statutes, the President may: seize property; organize and control the means of production; seize commodities; assign military forces abroad; institute martial law; seize and control all transportation and communication; regulate the operation of private enterprise; restrict travel; and in a plethora of particular ways, control the lives of all American citizens . . . A majority of the people of the United States have lived all of their lives under emergency rule. For 40 years, freedoms and governmental procedures guaranteed by the Constitution have in varying degrees been abridged by laws brought into force by states of national emergency . . . "

In Reg: U.S. Senate Report No. 93-549 dated 11/19/73 (73 CIS Serial Set S963-2 – [607 Pages]

"What is called 'proclaiming martial law' is no law at all; but merely for the sake of public safety, in circumstances of great emergency, setting aside all law, and acting under military power..."

8 Atty. Gen. Op. 365, 367, February 3, 1857.

And the Magna Carta is full of evidence of martial law rule being imposed in England, including but not limited to;

    i.   Chapter 13 where they were charging fees, and harassing people (customs), under the color of law (Martial Law), to enter into the City of London (foreign territory) under the second part of Chapter 13.

"And the city of London shall have all its ancient liberties and free customs, as well by land as by water; furthermore, we decree and grant that all other cities,

13

boroughs, towns, and ports, shall have all their liberties and free customs. " [emphasis added]

ii.   and Chapter 23 where their martial law shock troops, under the color of law (Martial Law dictatorship), were forcing people and villages to build bridges;
"No village or individual shall be compelled to make bridges at river banks, except those who from of old were legally bound to do so."

iii.   and Chapter 24 where their martial law shock troops, were holding hearings without a judge, under the color of law (Martial Law dictatorship), and is EXACTLY what they do when their hired thugs unlawfully arrest you on the road today;
"No sheriff, constable, coroners, or others of our bailiffs, shall hold pleas of our Crown."

iv.   and Chapter 28 where their martial law shock troops were stealing corn and other provisions under the color of law (Fascist PAPAL Martial Law dictatorship), without paying for it.
"No constable or other bailiff of ours shall take corn or other provisions from anyone without immediately tendering money therefor, unless he can have postponement thereof by permission of the seller."

v.   and Chapter 30 where the martial law shock troops were stealing horses and carts based on their trumped up charges for transport duty, under the color of law (PAPAL Fascist Martial Law dictatorship);
"No sheriff or bailiff of ours, or other person, shall take

the horses or carts of any freeman for transport duty, against the will of the said freeman."

vi.   and Chapter 31 where the martial law shock troops were stealing wood under the color of law (Martial Law dictatorship);
"Neither we nor our bailiffs shall take, for our castles or for any other work of ours, wood which is not ours, against the will of the owner of that wood."

vii.   and Chapter 38, where they were imposing their Private PAPAL Fascist Martial Law upon the people under the color of law (Martial Law dictatorship) which is exactly what they do when their hired thugs issue a "citation" or traffic ticket, or their hired thugs stop you at the so-called border;
"No bailiff for the future shall, upon his own unsupported complaint, put anyone to his "law", without credible witnesses brought for their purposes."

viii.   and Chapter 39 where they were imprisoning people, stealing their property, violating their rights under the color of law (Martial Law dictatorship);
"No freemen shall be taken or imprisoned or disseised or exiled or in any way destroyed, nor will we go upon him nor send upon him, except by the lawful judgment of his peers or by the law of the land."

ix.   and Chapter 40 where they were charging fees for their so-called justice, (filing fees, and other fees and regulations), denying access to justice by making rules, regulations and fees, under the color of law (PAPAL

Fascist Martial Law dictatorship), and this is all going on today in their so-called courts, at the hands of judicial whores who intend to sell their so-called justice;

"To no one will we sell, to no one will we refuse or delay, right or justice."

     x.   and Chapter 45 where officers of the court, and other officials were ignoring the law and violating the rights of the people under the color of law (Martial Law dictatorship), and this Chapter was inserted to create the presumption that the officers of the court and other officers are presumed to know the law;

"We will appoint as justices, constables, sheriffs, or bailiffs only such as know the law of the realm and mean to observe it well."

     xi.   and Chapter 55 they were imposing fines, and other sentences under the color of law (PAPAL Fascist Martial Law dictatorship);

"All fines made with us unjustly and against the law of the land, and all amercements, imposed unjustly and against the law of the land, shall be entirely remitted ....",

and martial law is under the Vatican's Roman Law, because civil law, and Roman Law, and Municipal Law are convertible phrases

"Civil Law," "Roman Law," and "Roman Civil Law" are convertible phrases, meaning the same system of jurisprudence. That rule of action which every particular nation, commonwealth, or city has established peculiarly for itself; more properly called "municipal"

law, to distinguish it from the "law of nature," and from international law." — See Bowyer, Mod. Civil Law, 19; Sevier v. Riley, 189 Cal. 170, 244 P. 323, 325" Black's Law Dictionary, Rev. 4th Ed.

"Admiralty Law. The terms "admiralty" and "maritime" law are virtually synonymous." — Black's Law Dictionary 6th Ed. 1990

"Civil Law, that rule of action which every particular nation, commonwealth or city has established peculiarly for itself, more properly distinguished by the name of municipal law." — The Dictionary of English Law, Sweet and Maxwell Ltd., London, 1959.

"There must be uniformity in maritime law; the principles of maritime laws are applicable to commercial law, and therefore, there must be uniformity in the commercial law." — Swift v. Tyson, 16 Pet 1, (1842)

"And the forms and modes of proceedings in causes of equity, and of admiralty, and maritime jurisdiction, shall be according to the civil law." — Wayman and another v. Southard and another, 10 Wall 1, p. 317,

and under the Vatican's Concordat, the wearing of clerical dress or of a religious habit by someone not authorized is punished by death by firing squad, because in the military, such people are treated as spies, and summarily executed, which is further proof that martial law comes under Roman law from the Vatican

"The wearing of clerical dress or of a religious habit by

17

lay people, or by members of the clergy or religious orders by whom this use is forbidden by a definitive and legally valid directive of the competent ecclesiastical authority and officially communicated to the state authority, is liable to the same penalty by the state as the misuse of the military uniform." — Article 10, 1933 Concordat with the Vatican [emphasis added]

and the objective was for martial law rule to eliminate common law and one of the ways they do that is by seizing all of the gold.

"It is an established fact that the United States Federal Government has been dissolved by the Emergency Banking Act, March 9, 1933, 48 stat. 1, Public Law 89-719; declared by President Roosevelt, being bankrupt and insolvent, H.J.R. 192, 73rd Congress in session June 5, 1933 – Joint Resolution To Suspend The Gold Standard and Abrogate The Gold Clause dissolved the Sovereign Authority of the United States and the official capacities of all United States Governmental Offices, Officers, and Departments and is further evidence that the United States Federal Government exists today in name only." — United States Congressional Record, March 17, 1993 Vol. 33 [Emphasis added],

because at common law ONLY gold or silver coin is legal tender.

"At common law only gold and silver were a legal tender. (2 Inst. 577.)" — McClarin v. Nesbit, 2 Nott & McC. (11 S.C.L.) 519 (1820),

and while they could NOT completely eliminate gold or

18

silver coin, they could compel all of their bankster owned and operated corporate commercial thugs to use their IOU's, Federal Reserve Notes, which they did with the Gold Reserve Act of 1934.

"Sec. 15. As used in this Act the term "United States" means the Government of the United States... the term "currency of the United States" means currency which is legal tender in the United States, and includes United States notes,... Federal Reserve Notes..." — Gold Reserve Act of 1934, 48 Stat. 337,

which technically says that Federal Reserve Notes (IOU's) are meant for internal government use ONLY, but because all corporations are subject to government regulations, they are also agencies of the government, and they are compelled to use Federal Reserve Notes as well, and Federal Reserve Notes are "legal tender", and are therefore forced loans.

"The forced loans of 1862 and 1863, in the form of legal tender notes, were vital forces in the struggle for national supremacy. They formed a part of the public debt of the United States..." — Julliard v. Greenman, 110 US 432.

and Federal Reserve Notes are also Bills of Credit;
"The said notes shall be obligations of the United States."
— 12 USC § 411 [Emphasis added]

and Federal Reserve Notes are NOT promissory Notes, because there is no promise to pay, therefore they can ONLY be IOU's;

"PROMISSORY NOTE, contracts. A written promise to pay a certain sum of money, at a future time, uncondi-

tionally." — 7 Watts & S. 264; 2 Humph. R. 143; 10 Wend. 675; Minor, R. 263; 7 Misso. 42; 2 Cowen, 536; 6 N. H. Rep. 364; 7 Vern. 22.

"A promissory note differs from a mere acknowledgment of debt, without any promise to pay, as when the debtor gives his creditor an I 0 U. (q. v.) See 2 Yerg. 50; 15 M. & W. 23. But see 2 Humph. 143; 6 Alab. R. 373." — Bouvier's Law Dictionary, 1856 Edition [Emphasis added]

and anyone who uses Federal Reserve Notes to purchase something is using United States, Inc. credit, and they are saying that they are a United States Citizen, and a United States citizen is a fraud, and a fictitious entity and a slave as described in the Corporate Denial Affidavit # 062013 which is recorded with the Pinal County Recorder at Fee Number 2013-032373, and all subsequent superseding documents, *all of which is incorporated herein by reference in its entirety, and all of which is now the un-rebutted truth and public policy,* and,

they are saying that they are a pauper because they are using IOU's to purchase something,

"The better to secure and perpetuate mutual friendship and intercourse among the people of the different States in this Union, the free inhabitants of each of these States, paupers, vagabonds, and fugitives from justice excepted, shall be entitled to all privileges and immunities of free citizens in the several States; and the people of each State shall have free ingress and regress to and from any other State..." — Article IV of the Articles of Confederation.

and at common law a pauper has no rights,

"Pauper – One so poor he must be supported at the public expense." — Bouvier's Law Dictionary 1856 Edition.

"Pauper. A very poor person, esp. one who receives aid from charity or public funds." — Black's Law Dictionary 8th Edition, and,

the United States, Inc., owns whatever was purchased, which is why there is a tax (tribute), and since the bankster thieves own the United States, Inc., as described in the Corporate Denial Affidavit # 062013 which is recorded with the Pinal County Recorder at Fee Number 2013-032373, and all subsequent superseding documents, *all of which is incorporated herein by reference in its entirety, and all of which is now the un-rebutted truth and public policy,* they have effectively stolen everything,

and the big reason they wanted to eliminate common law is because there is no common law judicial immunity, and they intend that their BAR member judicial thugs have immunity for the crimes that their Vatican handlers intend that they commit;
"There is no common law judicial immunity." — Pulliam v. Allen, 104 S.Ct. 1970,

and there is no qualified immunity, or any other immunity, at common law, for their color of law code enforcers, that their BAR member owned and operated corporate commercial de facto so-called courts have given them,

and as they intended, their martial law rule eliminated common law when it precipitated the War of Independence, just as it eliminates common law today;

"In the meantime, "Civil Law" was the form of law imposed in the Roman Empire which was largely (if not wholly) governed by martial law rule. "Equity" has always been understood to follow the law; to have "superior equity," is to turn things on their head. This is exactly what happens when martial law is imposed. If "equity" is the law, then it follows its own course rather than following the common law, thereby destroying the common law and leaving what is called "equity" in its place."
— Dyett v. Turner, 439 P2d 266 @ 269, 20 U2d 403 [1968] The Non-Ratification of the Fourteenth Amendment by Assistant Director A.H. Ellett, Utah Supreme Court.

"...statutes have been passed extending the courts of admiralty and vice-admiralty far beyond their ancient limits for depriving us the accustomed and inestimable privilege of trial by jury, in cases affecting both life and property... to supersede the course of common law and instead thereof to publish and order the use and exercise of the law martial... and for altering fundamentally the form of government established by charter. We saw the misery to which such despotism [military dictatorship] would reduce us." — Causes and Necessity for Taking Up Arms (1775).

"That the respective colonies are entitled to the common law of England, and more especially to the great and inestimable privilege of being tried by their peers of the vicinage, according to the course of that law.
Resolved, That the following acts of Parliament are infringements and violations of the rights of the colonists;

and that the repeal of them is essentially necessary, in order to restore harmony between Great Britain and the American colonies, viz.:
The several Acts of 4 Geo. 3, ch. 15 & ch. 34; 5 Geo. 3, ch. 25; 6 Geo. 3, ch. 52; 7 Geo. 3, ch. 41 & 46; 8 Geo. 3, ch. 22; which impose duties for the purpose of raising a revenue in America, extend the powers of the admiralty courts beyond their ancient limits, deprive the American subject of trial by jury, authorize the judges' certificate to indemnify the prosecutor from damages that he might otherwise be liable to, requiring oppressive security from a claimant of ships and goods seized before he shall be allowed to defend his property; and are subversive of American rights." — Declaration and Resolves of the First Continental Congress (October 1774)

and the foreign enemy agent BAR members in the legislatures and US Congress know that common law is eliminated, because they pass statutes for common law crimes, like the common law crime of misprision of felony.
"MISPRISION OF FELONY. The offense of concealing a felony committed by another, but without such previous concert with or subsequent assistance to the felon as would make the party concealing an accessory before or after the fact." — 4 Steph.Comm. 260; 4 Bl.Comm. 121; United States v. Perlstein, C.C.A.N.J., 126 F.2d 789, 798."
Black's Law Dictionary 4th Edition, page 1152
which is codified at 18 USC § 4,
"Whoever, having knowledge of the actual commission of a felony cognizable by a court of the United States, conceals and does not as soon as possible make known

23

the same to some judge or other person in civil or military authority under the United States, shall be fined under this title or imprisoned not more than three years, or both." — 18 USC § 4,

and the common law crime of barratry,
"No action can be taken against a sovereign in the non-constitutional courts of either the United States or the state courts & any such action is considered the crime of Barratry. Barratry is an offense at common law." — State vs. Batson, 17 S.E. 2d 511, 512, 513.

"(a) A person commits an offense if, with intent to obtain an economic benefit the person:
(1) knowingly institutes a suit or claim that the person has not been authorized to pursue;
(d) A person commits an offense if the person:
(1) is an attorney, chiropractor, physician, surgeon, or private investigator licensed to practice in this state or any person licensed, certified, or registered by a health care regulatory agency of this state; and..." — Texas Penal Code Section 38.12. BARRATRY AND SOLICITATION OF PROFESSIONAL EMPLOYMENT, [emphasis added],

and they have to pass statutes making common law the rule of decision
"The rule of decision in this state consists of those portions of the common law of England that are not inconsistent with the constitution or the laws of this state, the constitution of this state, and the laws of this state." — Texas Civil and Practice Code. Section 5.001 Rule of De-

24

cision [Emphasis added]

when they know that common law is already the law of the land, and has always been the law of the land, and will always be the law of the land

"...the individual may stand upon his constitutional rights as a Citizen. He is entitled to carry on his private business in his own way. His power to contract is unlimited. He owes no duty to the state or to his neighbors to divulge his business, or to open his doors to an investigation, so far as it may tend to incriminate him. He owes no such duty to the state, since he receives nothing therefrom, beyond the protection of his life, liberty, and property. His rights are such as existed by the law of the land long antecedent to the organization of the state, and can only be taken from him by due process of law, and in accordance with the Constitution. Among his rights are a refusal to incriminate himself, and the immunity of himself and his property from arrest or seizure except under (a judicial power warrant) a warrant of the law. He owes nothing to the public so long as he does not trespass upon their rights." — Hale v. Henkel, 201 U.S. 43

because under Martial Law Rule, there are no crimes, and they conveniently forget to make statutes for common law crimes, like infanticide, because the BAR members in the legislatures and US Congress intend to support the Vatican's policy of population reduction, and then the BAR members in the Supreme Court come out with rulings allowing their US citizen slaves to murder their unborn children

"The unborn are not included within the definition of "person" as used in the 14th Amendment." Roe v. Wade, US Supreme Court, 410 US 13, 35L. Ed. 2d 147, 1973

which also exposes the BAR members agenda to commit genocide against state citizens in America, because if the unborn are NOT a "person", they are murdering state citizens who are also NOT a "person" as described in the Corporate Denial Affidavit # 062013 which is recorded with the Pinal County Recorder at Fee Number 2013-032373, and all subsequent superseding documents, *all of which is incorporated herein by reference in its entirety, and all of which is now the un-rebutted truth, and public policy,*

which is the exact same reason for the War of Independence, and evidence of that fact is found in the Causes and Necessity of Taking Up Arms (1775), Declaration and Resolves of the First Continental Congress (October 1774), and the Declaration of Independence (1776);

"We hold these truths to be self-evident, that all men are created equal, that they are endowed by their Creator with certain unalienable Rights, that among these are Life, Liberty and the pursuit of Happiness.–That to secure these rights, Governments are instituted among Men, deriving their just powers from the consent of the governed, —That whenever any Form of Government becomes destructive of these ends, it is the Right of the People to alter or to abolish it, and to institute new Government, laying its foundation on such principles and organizing its powers in such form, as to them shall seem most likely to effect their Safety and Happiness. ... But

when a long train of abuses and usurpations, pursuing invariably the same Object evinces a design to reduce them under absolute Despotism, [military dictatorship] *it is their right, it is their duty, to throw off such Government, and to provide new Guards for their future security.–.... The history of the present King of Great Britain is a history of repeated injuries and usurpations, all having in direct object the establishment of an absolute Tyranny* [military dictatorship] *over these States. To prove this, let Facts be submitted to a candid world.*

-He has affected to render the Military independent of and superior to the Civil power. [military dictatorship]

-He has combined with others to subject us to a jurisdiction foreign to our constitution, [military dictatorship] and unacknowledged by our laws; giving his Assent to their Acts of pretended Legislation: [color of law]

For protecting them, by a mock Trial, [military dictatorship] from punishment for any Murders which they should commit on the Inhabitants of these States:

For imposing Taxes on us without our Consent: [military dictatorship]

For depriving us in many cases, of the benefits of Trial by Jury: [military dictatorship]

For transporting us beyond Seas to be tried for pretended offences [color of law – military dictatorship]

For abolishing the free System of English Laws in a neighbouring Province, establishing therein an Arbitrary government, [military dictatorship] *and enlarging its Boundaries so as to render it at once an example and fit instrument for introducing the same absolute rule* [military dictatorship] *into these Colonies:*

For taking away our Charters, abolishing our most valuable Laws, and altering fundamentally the Forms of our Governments: [military dictatorship]
He has abdicated Government here, by declaring us out of his Protection and waging War against us. [military dictatorship]" — Declaration of Independence 1776 [emphasis added]

and the Crown's BAR members are used to enforce their martial law rule, and further,

The founding fathers knew about the danger that the BAR members of the Crown posed in support of the military dictatorship, and the things that would be necessary to bring about the military dictatorship and they tried to prevent BAR members from being able to hold any position of trust (requires an oath of office) with;

"No state without the Consent of the united states in congress assembled, shall send any embassy to, or receive any embassy from, or enter into any conference, agreement, or alliance or treaty with any King prince or state; nor shall any person holding any office of profit or trust under the united states, or any of them, accept of any present, emolument, office or title of any kind whatever from any king, prince or foreign state; nor shall the united states in congress assembled, or any of them, grant any title of nobility."
Article IV, Articles of Confederation [emphasis added]

"No Title of Nobility shall be granted by the United States: And no Person holding any Office of Profit or Trust under them, shall, without the Consent of the Congress,

accept of any present, Emolument, Office, or Title, of any kind whatever, from any King, Prince, or foreign State." — Constitution for the United States of America, Article I, Section 9, Clause 8 [emphasis added]

and they continued to have BAR member problems, because they further ratified the true Article Thirteen in Amendment which says;

"If any citizen of the United States shall accept, claim, receive, or retain any title of nobility or honor, or shall, without the consent of congress, accept and retain any present, pension, office, or emolument of any kind whatever, from any emperor, king, prince, or foreign power, such person shall cease to be a citizen of the United States, and shall be incapable of holding any office of trust or profit under them, or either of them." [Emphasis added]

as taken from a certified copy of an 1819 Constitution for the United States of America, taken from Virginia Statutes, a true copy of which is attached to the Affidavit of Criminal Complaint 04/14/07 which is recorded with the Pinal County Recorder at Fee Number 2007-059087, and the Affidavit of Criminal Complaint 06/14/07 which is recorded with the Pinal County Recorder at Fee Number 2007-073069, all of both of which are incorporated herein by reference in their entirety, and all BAR members receive an honor from a foreign power based in London, England, and the City of London is a foreign state, as described herein;

"TITLE, persons. Titles are distinctions by which a person is known. 3. The constitution of the United States

29

forbids the tyrant by the United States, or any state of any title of nobility. (q. v.)... judges and members of congress that of honorable; and members of the bar and justices of the peace are called esquires. Cooper's, Justinian, 416'; Brackenridge's Law Miscell. Index." — Bouvier's Law Dictionary 1856 Edition, [emphasis added],

and all BAR members receive a Title of Nobility
"NOBILITAS EST DUPLEX, SUPERIOR ET INFERIOR. 2 Inst. 583. There are two sorts of nobility, the higher and the lower."
Black's Law Dictionary 4th Edition, page 1198 [emphasis added],

"ESQUIRE. A title applied by courtesy to officers of almost every description, to members of the bar, and others. 2. In England, it is a title next above that of a gentleman, and below a knight." — Bouvier's Law Dictionary 1856 Edition, [emphasis added], and further,

Every state has a State BAR, which is governed by the state Supreme Court,
"(a) The Board of Law Examiners, acting under instructions of the supreme court as provided by this chapter, shall determine the eligibility of candidates for examination for a license to practice law in this state." — Texas Government Code Section 82.004 Board Duties [emphasis added]

"In this subchapter:
(4) "State agency" includes:
(A) a department, commission, board, office, or other

state governmental entity in the executive or legislative branch of state government;

(B) the Supreme Court of Texas, the Court of Criminal Appeals of Texas, a court of appeals, the Texas Judicial Council, the Office of Court Administration of the Texas Judicial System, the State Bar of Texas, or any other state governmental entity in the judicial branch of state government;

(C) a university system or an institution of higher education as defined by Section 61.003, Education Code; and

(D) any other state governmental entity that the comptroller determines to be a component unit of state government for the purpose of financial reporting under Section 403.013."

Texas Government Code Section 403.241 Definitions

and there are statutes requiring all judges to be BAR members,

"(a) A municipal court of record is presided over by one or more municipal judges.

(b) The governing body shall by ordinance appoint its municipal judges.

(c) A municipal judge must:

(1) be a resident of this state;

(2) be a citizen of the United States;

(3) be a licensed attorney in good standing; and

(4) have two or more years of experience in the practice of law in this state."

Texas Government Code Section 30.00006 JUDGE [emphasis added]

"To qualify for appointment as an associate judge under this subchapter, a person must:
(1) be a resident of this state and one of the counties the person will serve;
(2) have been licensed to practice law in this state for at least four years;"
Texas Government Code Section 54A.003 Qualifications [emphasis added]

and even federal judges are BAR members
"No individual may be appointed or reappointed to serve as a magistrate judge under this chapter unless: (1) He has been for at least five years a member in good standing of the bar of..." — 28 USC § 631(b)(1)

and all prosecutors are BAR members;
"(a) An assistant prosecuting attorney must be licensed to practice law in this state and shall take the constitutional oath of office." — Texas Government Code Section 41.103 Assistant Prosecuting Attorneys [emphasis added]

and the Court of Criminal Appeals of Texas, the various Courts of Appeals, the Texas Judicial Council, the Office of Court Administration of the Texas Judicial System, the State Bar of Texas and the Judiciary Courts of the State of Texas, Inc., and its parent corporation State of Texas, Inc., as found in the Affidavit of Daniel-Lee: Swank which is recorded with the Liberty County Recorder at Recording # 2008010522, a true copy of which is attached hereto, *all of which is incorporated herein by reference in its entirety which is now "public policy",* and they are all unconstitutional delegations of authority;

"The governments are but trustees acting under derived authority and have no power to delegate what is not delegated to them. But the people, as the original fountain might take away what they have delegated and entrust to whom they please. ... The sovereignty in every state resides in the people of the state and they may alter and change their form of government at their own pleasure." — Luther v. Borden, 48 US 1, 12 Led 581

"A delegate cannot delegate; an agent cannot delegate his functions to a subagent without the knowledge or consent of the principal; the person to whom an office or duty is delegated cannot lawfully devolve the duty on another, unless he be expressly authorized so to do." — 9 Coke, 77; Broom, Max. 840; 2 Kent, Comm. 633; 2 Steph. Comm. 119 [emphasis added]

"A delegated power cannot be again delegated." — 2 Inst. 597; Black's, 2d. 347; 2 Bouv. Inst. n. 1300

"A deputy cannot have (or appoint) a deputy." — Story, Ag. s.13; 9 Coke, 77; 2 Bouv. Inst. n. 1936,

therefore they have no authority,

"An unconstitutional act is not law; it confers no rights; it imposes no duties; affords no protection; it creates no office; it is in legal contemplation, as inoperative as though it had never been passed." — Norton vs Shelby County, 118 U.S. 425, p. 442

and they are all criminal racketeering enterprises,

"As used in this chapter—

"(1) "racketeering activity" means

(A) any act or threat involving murder, kidnapping, gambling, arson, robbery, bribery, extortion, ... which is chargeable under State law and punishable by imprisonment for more than one year;

(B) any act which is indictable under any of the following provisions of title 18, United States Code: section 1341 (relating to mail fraud), section 1503 (relating to obstruction of justice), ...sections 1581–1592 (relating to peonage, slavery, and trafficking in persons)., section 1951 (relating to interference with commerce, robbery, or extortion), section 1952 (relating to racketeering), section 1957 (relating to engaging in monetary transactions in property derived from specified unlawful activity), sections 2421–24 (relating to white slave traffic),..."

— 18 USC § 1961

"(a) Whoever, as consideration for the receipt of, or as consideration for a promise or agreement to pay, anything of pecuniary value from an enterprise engaged in racketeering activity, or for the purpose of gaining entrance to or maintaining or increasing position in an enterprise engaged in racketeering activity, murders, kidnaps, maims, assaults with a dangerous weapon, commits assault resulting in serious bodily injury upon, or threatens to commit a crime of violence against any individual in violation of the laws of any State or the United States, or attempts or conspires so to do, shall be punished." — 18 USC § 1959

and they and their hired thugs are criminal street gangs;

"(a)   "Combination" means three or more persons who collaborate in carrying on criminal activities, although:
(1)   participants may not know each other's identity;
(2)   membership in the combination may change from time to time; and
(3)   participants may stand in a wholesaler-retailer or other arm's-length relationship in illicit distribution operations.
(b)   "Conspires to commit" means that a person agrees with one or more persons that they or one or more of them engage in conduct that would constitute the offense and that person and one or more of them perform an overt act in pursuance of the agreement. An agreement constituting conspiring to commit may be inferred from the acts of the parties.
(c)   "Profits" means property constituting or derived from any proceeds obtained, directly or indirectly, from an offense listed in Section 71.02.
(d)   "Criminal street gang" means three or more persons having a common identifying sign or symbol or an identifiable leadership who continuously or regularly associate in the commission of criminal activities." Texas Penal Code Title 11. Organized Crime, Chapter 71. Organized Crime § 71.01
"(a)   A person commits an offense if, with the intent to establish, maintain, or participate in a combination or in the profits of a combination or as a member of a criminal street gang, the person commits or conspires to commit one or more of the following:
(1)   murder, capital murder, arson, aggravated robbery, robbery, burglary, theft, aggravated kidnapping, kidnapping, aggravated assault, aggravated sexual assault,

sexual assault, forgery, deadly conduct, assault punish-
able as a Class A misdemeanor, burglary of a motor ve-
hicle, or unauthorized use of a motor vehicle;
(8) any felony offense under Chapter 32;
(9) any offense under Chapter 36;
(11) any offense under Section 37.11(a);
(12) any offense under Chapter 20A;
(13) any offense under Section 37.10;
(14) any offense under Section 38.06, 38.07, 38.09, or
38.11;
(15) any offense under Section 42.10;
(16) any offense under Section 46.06(a)(1) or 46.14; or
(17) any offense under Section 20.05."
Texas Penal Code Title 11. Organized Crime, Chapter 71.
Organized Crime § 71.01, and further,

The BAR member judicial thugs intend to compel
their BAR member "representation" by one of their BAR
member buddies, so they can force their foreign jurisdiction upon their victim;
"IN PROPRIA PERSONA. In one's own proper person.
It is a rule in pleading that pleas to the jurisdiction of the
court must be plead in propria persona, because if pleaded
by attorney they admit the jurisdiction, as an attorney is
an officer of the court, and he is presumed to plead after
having obtained leave, which admits the jurisdiction."
Lawes, Pl. 91." Black's Law Dictionary, 4th Edition, page
899-900

where their so-called justice is a fraud;
"He is however in a sense an officer of the state with an
obligation to the Court...His first duty is to the courts

36

and to the public, not to the client, and whenever his duties to his client conflict with those as an officer of the court, in the administration of justice, the former must yield to the latter." — 7 Corpus Juris Secundum § 4 Attorneys [emphasis added]

so they can convert their victim into a ward of the court; *"Clients are also called "wards of the court..."* — 7 Corpus Juris Secundum § 4 Attorneys

and a ward of the court is an imbecile, *"Wards of court. Infants and persons of unsound mind. Davis' Committee v. Loney, 290 Ky. 644, 162 S.W.2d 189, 190. Their rights must be guarded jealously. Montgomery v. Erie R. Co., C.C.A.N.J., 97 F.2d 289, 292."* Blacks Law Dictionary, 4th Edition, page 1755 [emphasis added]

and these BAR members intend to criminally convert their victim into one of their wards of the court so the BAR member thugs on the bench can collect their royalties, and violate their victims rights with impunity, and put them in the warehouse (jail), and their thieving bankster buddies can get rich too, *"(a) The controlling rule is that "absent a knowing and intelligent waiver, no person may be imprisoned for any offense . . . unless he was represented by counsel at his trial."* — Argersinger, 407 U. S., at 37. Pp. 5–6." Alabama v Shelton 535 U.S. 654

"...when the trial of a misdemeanor starts no imprisonment may be imposed, even though local law permits it,

unless the accused is represented by counsel."
— Argersinger v. Hamlin, 407 U S 25, 40 (1971),

and according to Earl Warren, former Chief Judge, US Supreme Court, BAR members are either incompetent or criminals,
"Between 75% to 90% of all lawyers are either incompetent, dishonest, or both."
— Earl Warren (former) Chief Justice US Supreme Court,

and the practice of law is an occupation of common right, but BAR members intend to deprive the people of that right, as evidenced herein,
"The practice of Law can not be licensed by any state/ State." — Schware v. Board of Examiners, 353 U.S. 238, 239 [emphasis added]

"The practice of Law is an occupation of common right."
— Sims v. Aherns, 71 S.W. 720 (1925), and further,

BAR members criminally convert your name under their Roman Law
"Capitis Diminutio (meaning the diminishing of status through the use of capitalization) In Roman law. A diminishing or abridgment of personality; a loss or curtailment of a man's status or aggregate of legal attributes and qualifications."

"Capitis Diminutio Maxima (meaning a maximum loss of status through the use of capitalization, e.g. JOHN DOE or DOE JOHN) – The highest or most comprehensive loss of status. This occurred when a man'scondition

was changed from one of freedom to one of bondage, when he became a slave. It swept away with it all rights of citizenship and all family rights. " — Black's Law Dictionary 4th Edition [emphasis added]

to fabricate evidence that you are a corporation (US citizen/slave) as described in the Corporate Denial Affidavit # 062013 which is recorded with the Pinal County Recorder at Fee Number 2013-032373, and all subsequent superseding documents, all of which is incorporated herein by reference in its entirety, and all of which is now the unrebutted truth, and public policy, because a corporation is property, and property has no rights, and they intend to violate your rights in every way possible, and that is exactly what they do, with they make unlawful legal determinations for you, and unlawfully represent you, and it is deliberate, and calculated, and intentional, and further,

The Constitution for the United States of America is the supreme law of the land,
"This Constitution, and the Laws of the United States which shall be made in Pursuance thereof; and all Treaties made, or which shall be made, under the Authority of the United States, shall be the supreme Law of the Land; and the Judges in every State shall be bound thereby, any Thing in the Constitution or Laws of any State to the Contrary notwithstanding." — US Constitution, Article 6, Clause 2

therefore under the true Article Thirteen in Amendment,
"If any citizen of the United States shall accept, claim, receive, or retain any title of nobility or honor, or shall,

without the consent of congress, accept and retain any present, pension, office, or emolument of any kind whatever, from any emperor, king, prince, or foreign power, such person shall cease to be a citizen of the United States, and shall be incapable of holding any office of trust or profit under them, or either of them." [Emphasis added]

no BAR member can hold a position of trust (requires an oath of office) therefore all judges (state or federal) are NOT judges, and have no authority, and are in fact criminals because they perjure their oath the moment they take it, and the BAR members in the legislature give them immunity which was complained about in;

"That the respective colonies are entitled to the common law of England, and more especially to the great and inestimable privilege of being tried by their peers of the vicinage, according to the course of that law.
Resolved, That the following acts of Parliament are infringements and violations of the rights of the colonists; and that the repeal of them is essentially necessary, in order to restore harmony between Great Britain and the American colonies, viz.:
The several Acts of 4 Geo. 3, ch. 15 & ch. 34; 5 Geo. 3, ch. 25; 6 Geo. 3, ch. 52; 7 Geo. 3, ch. 41 & 46; 8 Geo. 3, ch. 22; which impose duties for the purpose of raising a revenue in America, extend the powers of the admiralty courts beyond their ancient limits, deprive the American subject of trial by jury, authorize the judges' certificate to indemnify the prosecutor from damages that he might otherwise be liable to, requiring oppressive security from a claimant of ships and goods seized before he shall be

allowed to defend his property; and are subversive of American rights." — Declaration and Resolves of the First Continental Congress (October 1774)

and because the state legislatures and the US Congress are full of BAR members, they have no authority,
"it never became a law and was as much a nullity as if it had been the act or declaration of an unauthorized assemblage of individuals." — Ryan v. Lynch, 68 Ill. 160.

therefore, they are also criminals, and the United States, Inc., CEO, Barak Obama is a BAR member, therefore he is also a criminal, and the Declaration and Resolves of the First Continental Congress (October 1774) are being denied by these BAR members;
"Whereupon the deputies so appointed being now assembled, in a full and free representation of these Colonies, taking into their most serious consideration the best means of attaining the ends aforesaid, do in the first place, as Englishmen their ancestors in like cases have usually done, for asserting and vindicating their rights and liberties, declare,
That the inhabitants of the English Colonies in North America, by the immutable laws of nature, the principles of the English constitution, and the several charters or compacts, have the following Rights:
That our ancestors, who first settled these colonies, were at the time of their emigration from the mother country, entitled to all the rights, liberties, and immunities of free and natural born subjects within the realm of England. That by such emigration they by no means forfeited, surrendered, or lost any of those rights, but that they were,

41

and their descendants now are entitled to the exercise and enjoyment of all such of them, as their local and other circumstances enable them to exercise and enjoy. That the foundation of English liberty, and of all free government, is a right in the people to participate in their legislative council: and as the English colonists are not represented, and from their local and other circumstances, cannot properly be represented in the British parliament, they are entitled to a free and exclusive power of legislation in their several provincial legislatures, where their right of representation can alone be preserved, in all cases of taxation and internal polity, subject only to the negative of their sovereign, in such manner as has been heretofore used and accustomed. But, from the necessity of the case, and a regard to the mutual interest of both countries, we cheerfully consent to the operation of such acts of the British parliament, as are bona fide restrained to the regulation of our external commerce, for the purpose of securing the commercial advantages of the whole empire to the mother country, and the commercial benefits of its respective members excluding every idea of taxation, internal or external, for raising a revenue on the subjects in America without their consent.

That the respective colonies are entitled to the common law of England, and more especially to the great and inestimable privilege of being tried by their peers of the vicinage, according to the course of that law.

That they have a right peaceably to assemble, consider of their grievances, and petition the King; and that all prosecutions, prohibitory proclamations, and commitments for the same, are illegal." — Declaration and

Resolves of the First Continental Congress (October 1774),

and the right to petition the government for a redress of grievances is a reaffirmation of the Petition of Right which is taken from Chapter 61 of the Magna Carta;
"...and for the better allaying of the quarrel that has arisen between us and our barons,... and, laying the transgression before us, petition to have that transgression redressed without delay. And if we shall not have corrected the transgression...within forty days, reckoning from the time it has been intimated to us ...the four barons aforesaid shall refer that matter to the rest of the five and twenty barons, [grand jury] and those five and twenty barons shall, together with the community of the whole realm, distrain and distress us in all possible ways..." — Magna Carta Section 61 [Emphasis added],

and Chapter 40 of the Magna Carta which says;
"To no one will we sell, to no one will we refuse or delay, right or justice." — Magna Carta, Chapter 40

and the first ten amendments to The Constitution of the United States are a re-affirmation of common law rights *"History is clear that the first ten amendments to the Constitution were adopted to secure certain common law rights of the people, against invasion by the Federal Government."* — Bell v. Hood, 71 F.Supp., 813, 816 (1947) U.S.D.C. — So. Dist. CA. [emphasis added]

and the Petition of Right was re-affirmed in Article One in Amendment for the Constitution for the United States of

America and it has always been an unlimited and unregulatable right to Petition the government for a redress of grievances,

"Congress shall make no law .... abridging ..... the right of the people.... to petition the government for a redress of grievances."
Article 1 in Amendment, The Constitution of the United States

and for these judicial thugs to be selling their so-called justice is converting a right into a privilege;
"No State shall convert a liberty into a privilege, license it, and charge a fee therefore."
Murdock v. Pennsylvania, 319 US 105

"There can be no sanction or penalty imposed upon one because of this exercise of constitutional rights."
Sherer v. Cullen, 481 F 946

"If the State converts a right (liberty) *into a privilege, the citizen can ignore the license and fee and engage in the right* (liberty) *with impunity."*
Shuttlesworth v. City of Birmingham Alabama, 373 US 262:

and since the State of Texas, Inc., and its subsidiary Judiciary Courts of the State of Texas, Inc., are both federal municipal corporations, as described herein, the word "Congress" also means State of Texas, Inc., and Judiciary Courts of the State of Texas, Inc., and all of the BAR member benchers know this, because all officers of the court are presumed to know the law as described herein, and when I refuse to pay the extortion under color of office, *"Color of office. Pretense of official right to do act made by one who has no such right. Kiker v. Pinson, 120 Ga.App. 784, 172 S.E.2d 333, 334. An act under color of office is an act of an officer who claims authority to do the act by reason of his office when the office does not confer on him any such authority. Maryland Cas. Co. v. McCormack, Ky., 488 S.W.2d 347, 352."* Black's Law Dictionary 6th Edition, page 266 [emphasis added],

these BAR member judicial thugs deny their justice in violation of Chapter 40 of the Magna Carta which says; *"To no one will we sell, to no one will we refuse or delay, right or justice."* Magna Carta, Chapter 40

and their BAR member buddies in the legislature have even codified their extortion under color of office; *"The clerk of a district court shall collect fees and costs under the Local Government Code as follows:*
(1) additional filing fees:
(A) for each civil suit filed, for court-related purposes for the support of the judiciary and for civil legal services to an indigent:
(B) on the filing of any civil action or proceeding requiring a filing fee, including an appeal, and on the filing of any counterclaim, cross-action, intervention, interpleader, or third-party action requiring a filing fee, to fund civil legal services for the indigent:
(2) additional to fund the courthouse security fund, if authorized by the county commissioners court (Sec.

291.008, Local Government Code) . . . not to exceed $5;
(3) additional for filing documents not subject to certain filing fees to fund the courthouse security fund, if authorized by the county commissioners court (Sec. 291.008, Local Government Code) . . . $1;
(4) additional filing fee to fund the courthouse security fund in Webb County, if authorized by the county commissioners court (Sec. 291.009, Local Government Code) . . . not to exceed $20;
(5) court cost in civil cases other than suits for delinquent taxes to fund the county law library fund, if authorized by the county commissioners court (Sec. 323.023, Local Government Code) . . . not to exceed $35; and
(6) on the filing of a civil suit, an additional filing fee to be used for court-related purposes for the support of the judiciary (Sec. 133.154, Local Government Code) . . . $42."

Texas Government Code, Section 101.0615. District Court Fees and Costs

and all of this is coming from Wallace B. Jefferson, their current CEO Chief Judicial whore in the Supreme Court of Texas, as found in the Affidavit of Daniel-Lee: Swank which is recorded with the Liberty County Recorder at Recording # 2008010522, a true copy of which is attached hereto, all of which is incorporated herein by reference in its entirety, which is now "public policy", and;

"(a) The supreme court has the full rulemaking power in the practice and procedure in civil actions, except that its rules may not abridge, enlarge, or modify the substantive rights of a litigant.

(b) The supreme court from time to time may promulgate a specific rule or rules of civil procedure, or an amendment or amendments to a specific rule or rules, to be effective at the time the supreme court deems expedient in the interest of a proper administration of justice. The rules and amendments to rules remain in effect unless and until disapproved by the legislature. The clerk of the supreme court shall file with the secretary of state the rules or amendments to rules promulgated by the supreme court under this subsection and shall mail a copy of those rules or amendments to rules to each registered member of the State Bar of Texas not later than the 60th day before the date on which they become effective. On receiving a written request from a member of the legislature, the secretary of state shall provide the member with electronic notifications when the supreme court has promulgated rules or amendments to rules under this section.

(c) So that the supreme court has full rulemaking power in civil actions, a rule adopted by the supreme court repeals all conflicting laws and parts of laws governing practice and procedure in civil actions, but substantive law is not repealed. At the time the supreme court files a rule, the court shall file with the secretary of state a list of each article or section of general law or each part of an article or section of general law that is repealed or modified in any way. The list has the same weight and effect as a decision of the court.

(d) The rules of practice and procedure in civil actions shall be published in the official reports of the supreme court. The supreme court may adopt the method it deems expedient for the printing and distribution of the rules.

(f) The supreme court shall adopt rules governing the electronic filing of documents in civil cases in justice of the peace courts.

(g) The supreme court shall adopt rules to provide for the dismissal of causes of action that have no basis in law or fact on motion and without evidence. The rules shall provide that the motion to dismiss shall be granted or denied within 45 days of the filing of the motion to dismiss. The rules shall not apply to actions under the Family Code.

(h) The supreme court shall adopt rules to promote the prompt, efficient, and cost-effective resolution of civil actions. The rules shall apply to civil actions in district courts, county courts at law, and statutory probate courts in which the amount in controversy, inclusive of all claims for damages of any kind, whether actual or exemplary, a penalty, attorney's fees, expenses, costs, interest, or any other type of damage of any kind, does not exceed $100,000. The rules shall address the need for lowering discovery costs in these actions and the procedure for ensuring that these actions will be expedited in the civil justice system. The supreme court may not adopt rules under this subsection that conflict with a provision of:
(1) Chapter 74, Civil Practice and Remedies Code."
Government Code, Section 22.004 Rules of Civil Procedure

and they have no right to sell their so-called justice, and what they are doing is acting ultra vires of their authority, because they have no authority;

"Ultra vires. An act performed without any authority to act on subject. Haslund v. City of Seattle, 86 Wash.2d

607, 547 P.2d 1221, 1230. Acts beyond the scope of the powers of a corporation, as defined by its charter or laws of state of incorporation. State ex reI. v. Holston Trust Co., 168 Tenn. 546, 79 S.W.2d 1012, 1016. The term has a broad application and includes not only acts prohibited by the charter, but acts which are in excess of powers granted and not prohibited, and generally applied either when a corporation has no power whatever to do an act, or when the corporation has the power but exercises it irregularly. People ex reI. Barrett v. Bank of Peoria, 295 Ill.App. 543, 15 N.E.2d 333, 335. Act is ultra vires when corporation is without authority to perform it under any circumstances or for any purpose. By doctrine of ultra vires a contract made by a corporation beyond the scope of its corporate powers is unlawful. Community Federal Sav. & Loan Ass'n of Independence, Mo. v. Fields, C.C.A. Mo., 128 F.2d 705, 708. Ultra vires act of municipality is one which is beyond powers conferred upon it by law. Charles v. Town of Jeanerette, Inc., La.App., 234 So.2d 794, 798." Black's Law Dictionary 6th Edition page 1522, [emphasis added],

and Texas Rule of Civil Procedure are over 250 pages long, with over 600 rules, therefore they have absolutely nothing to do with justice and everything to do with lining their pockets, and denying justice as much as possible, and promoting their unconstitutional Texas State BAR, and the BAR members in the Texas Legislature have limited the liability of their municipal corporate thugs with their color of law Tort Claims Act that they intend to shove down everybody's throat, just like the judicial whore Cosby shoved it down My throat, when he limited the liability of

49

the Fort Worth PIGs, and released them from personal responsibility thereby, and all of this is to make sure that their corporate thugs continue to violate My rights, and the rights of everybody else, in support of their martial law military dictatorship, and the military occupation that has been going on since the civil war, and these judicial whores are NOT neutral or objective;

"It is a fundamental right of a party to have a neutral and detached judge preside over the judicial proceedings." — Ward v Village of Monroeville, 409 U.S. 57, 61-62, 93 S.Ct 80, 83, 34 L.Ed. 2d 267 (1972); Tumey v Ohio, 273 U.S. 510, 5209, 47 S. Ct. 437, 440, 71 L.Ed. 749 (1927)

because they intend to collect their extortion under color of office because it supports their so-called judiciary, as provided for by the BAR member thugs in the legislature, as described herein, just like the judicial whore Tom Lowe intended to collect his extortion under color of office in My case and the judicial whores in the Court of so-called Appeals dismissed the case for want of jurisdiction, a true copy of which is attached hereto, all of which is incorporated herein by reference in its entirety, and the judicial whore refused to put their name on it, because they intended to hide their identity, and these judicial whores intend to collect their extortion under color of office for their BAR member judicial whore buddy, Wallace B. Jefferson, CEO, Judiciary Courts of the State of Texas, Inc., just like Wilder, the ringleader of the judicial whores in Fort Worth, sent their fraudulently created strawman a bill for $1,979.00 for an Appeal in a case with another of Wilder's judicial whore buddies Cosby, a true copy of which is attached hereto, all of which is incorporated herein by reference in its entirety, and the judicial whores in the so-called Court of Appeals are denying their so-called justice until the extortion is paid, because they intend to deny any real justice to everybody except their BAR member buddies, even if they do pay their extortion, and that is Texas justice, where the judicial whore presumes the case before it even starts, and these judicial whores like Cosby, and Lowe intend to deprive everyone of any justice because it makes so much business for Jefferson, and his so-called courts,

"The power to create presumptions is not a means of escape from constitutional restrictions."
Bailey v Alabama, 219 U.S. 219, 238, et seq., 31 S.Ct. 145; Manley v Georgia, 279 U.S. 1, 5-6, 49 S.Ct. 215

and then these BAR members proceed to fabricate evidence to support the BAR member whore's presumption, and they after they break the bad news to you, the whores send you a bill for your "justice", and then they send their hired thugs out to assault you and kidnap you, until you pay their extortion, and this is a textbook criminal racketeering enterprise, as described herein, and they intend to perjure their oaths, because their BAR member buddies in the legislature have given them immunity, and your ONLY remedy is to go before one of their BAR member buddies, and further,

The BAR members in the legislature have admitted in their own statute that the Texas Code of Criminal Procedure is an unconstitutional act;
"The fact that the laws relating to criminal procedure in this state have not been completely revised and re-codified in more than a century past and the further fact that

the administration of justice, in the field of criminal law, has undergone changes, through judicial construction and interpretation of constitutional provisions, which have been, in certain instances, modified or nullified, as the case may be, necessitates important changes requiring the revision or modernization of the laws relating to criminal procedure, and the further fact that it is desirous and desirable to strengthen, and to conform, various provisions in such laws to current interpretation and application, emphasizes the importance of this legislation and all of which, together with the crowded condition of the calendar in both Houses, create an emergency and an imperative public necessity that the Constitutional Rule requiring bills to be read on three several days be suspended, and said Rule is hereby suspended, and that this Act shall take effect and be in force and effect from and after 12 o'clock Meridian on the 1st day of January, Anno Domini, 1966, and it is so enacted."

Texas Code of Criminal Procedure Article 54.03 Emergency Clause [emphasis added]

because emergency is NEVER justification for anything; *"Emergency does not create power. Emergency does not increase granted power or remove or diminish the restrictions imposed upon power granted or reserved. The Constitution was adopted in a period of grave emergency. Its grants of power to the Federal Government and its limitations of the power of the States were determined in the light of emergency, and they are not altered by emergency."*

Home Building and Loan Association v Blaisdel, 290 US 398 (1934) and the Texas Code of Criminal Procedure is an unconstitutional Act as described in the Corporate Denial Affidavit 062013 which is recorded with the Pinal County Recorder at Fee Number 2013-032373, and all subsequent superseding documents, all of which is incorporated herein by reference in its entirety, and all of which is now the unrebutted truth, and public policy, and the Texas Code of Criminal Procedure is color of law, and a fraud, and these BAR members use the Texas Code of Criminal Procedure to criminally convert everybody into their fraudulently created cestui que trust;

"(a) In alleging the name of a defendant corporation, it is sufficient to state in the complaint, indictment, or information the corporate name, or to state any name or designation by which the corporation is known or may be identified. It is not necessary to allege that the defendant was lawfully incorporated.

(b) In alleging the name of a defendant association it is sufficient to state in the complaint, indictment, or information the association's name, or to state any name or designation by which the association is known or may be identified, or to state the name or names of one or more members of the association, referring to the unnamed members as "others." It is not necessary to allege the legal form of the association."

Texas Code of Criminal Procedure Article 17A.02 Allegation of Name [emphasis added]

and these BAR members use their unconstitutional Texas Code of Criminal Procedure to send out their hired thugs to assault you, and kidnap you, based on a capias, and that is EXACTLY what has happened to people I know;

"(a) When a complaint is filed or an indictment or information presented against a corporation or association, the court or clerk shall issue a summons to the corporation or association. The summons shall be in the same form as a capias except that:

(1) it shall summon the corporation or association to appear before the court named at the place stated in the summons; and

(2) it shall be accompanied by a certified copy of the complaint, indictment, or information; and

(3) it shall provide that the corporation or association appear before the court named at or before 10 a.m. of the Monday next after the expiration of 20 days after it is served with summons, except when service is made upon the secretary of state or the Commissioner of Insurance, in which instance the summons shall provide that the corporation or association appear before the court named at or before 10 a.m. of the Monday next after the expiration of 30 days after the secretary of state or the Commissioner of Insurance is served with summons.

(b) Publicly Recorded at Pinal County Courthouse, Arizona

********** END ***********

"You Know Something is Wrong When…..An American Affidavit of Probable Cause"

http://tinyurl.com/hh2ug3u

You Know Something is Wrong When.....
An American Affidavit of Probable Cause

https://www.createspace.com/4390079
Password = *password*

Miscellaneous Writings
featuring Anna von Reitz

https://www.createspace.com/700022
Password = *password*

"As It Is The Truth"
by Judge Anna von Reitz

https://www.createspace.com/6470330
Password = *password*

Disclosure 101
What You Need To Know

https://www.createspace.com/4870915
Password = *password*

Rogue Sabre Special Ops
by Task-Force-Sheepdog

https://www.createspace.com/7053961
Password = *password*

Made in the USA
Las Vegas, NV
11 October 2021